Contents

The death of Diana, Princess of Wales, shocked the world.

1 A Shocking Death

It is just after midnight in Paris.
It is 31 August 1997, the end of the summer.
Diana and her new boyfriend, Dodi,
have just left the Ritz hotel in Paris.
They go out of the back door of the hotel.
Diana has never looked more beautiful.
Photographers are at the front of the hotel.

Diana, Dodi, the driver and the bodyguard
get into the black Mercedes.
The car speeds through the streets of Paris.
The car is going faster and faster.
They are trying to get away from
the photographers.
The photographers want more pictures
of Diana and Dodi together.

But the car is going too fast
as it enters an underpass.
It crashes straight into the wall.

The photographers are there taking pictures.
Diana is cut free from the car.
She is taken to hospital.
Four hours later, she is dead.

Before she died, Diana was
the most photographed woman
in the world.
People loved to read about her
and to see her picture.
It was not just because she was beautiful.

People liked her because
she cared about people.
She had a good, kind heart.
They liked her because she was honest.

The news of her death shocked the world.
In the week before the funeral,
millions of flowers were left
at her London home.
Thousands of people waited for hours
to write in the Books of Condolence.

Many people said they felt
as if they had lost a friend.
Tony Blair, the Prime Minister,
called her the 'People's Princess'.

On 6 September 1997, a million people
went to London to watch the funeral.
People from all walks of life
went to the service at Westminster Abbey.

Charity workers, artists, nurses and patients
sat next to the rich and famous.
Singers and film stars were also there –
George Michael, Tom Cruise, Tom Hanks, Sting.

Elton John sang for her.
His song, 'Candle in the Wind', sold more
than 31 million copies all over the world.

After the service, her coffin was driven
through the streets and out of London.
She was being taken back
to her childhood home.
Thousands of people lined the roads.

They came to say 'Goodbye'
to a woman they loved.
The death of this woman, at the age of 36,
had shocked the world.

But how did it all begin?
How did Diana touch
the lives of so many people?

2 Childhood

Diana was born on 1 July 1961
at Park House, Sandringham.
Her family was very rich
and her father had a title.
She had two older sisters, Sarah and Jane.
Her father had hoped that Diana
would be a boy.
Most of her childhood was at Park House.

But Diana's parents were not happy together.
In 1967, Diana's mother
fell in love with another man.
She left Diana's father.
Diana and her younger brother, Charles,
stayed with their father.

Diana's parents got divorced
when she was six years old.
Diana said later that she would hate
to get divorced.
She said that she didn't want her children
to go through the same pain.

Diana and her younger brother, Charles,
were very close.
They were looked after by nannies.
Diana's mother wanted her two young children,
Diana and Charles, to live with her.
But the court would not let her have them.

When Diana was nine years old,
she was sent away to school.
She found school work hard,
but she liked sports,
and helping to keep the school pets.
She won a prize for being kind to pets.

She liked going home in the school holidays
to see her brother.

Her grandfather died when she was 14.
This meant that Diana now had
the title 'Lady' before her name.
Diana, her brother and father
moved to Althorp house.
This was Diana's grandfather's house.

Diana had always cared about other people.

The house was on a very big estate.
There were beautiful gardens
and a lake with a small island.
Diana and her brother Charles
loved to play on the island.

Diana got on well with her father.
She loved him a lot.
However, when he married again,
he did not tell his children.
This made them very upset.
Diana, Charles and their two sisters
did not get on with their step-mother.
It took a few years before Diana and her
step-mother got on with each other.

Diana wasn't good at school work,
but she cared about her relationships
with people.
She had to take her GCSEs twice.
She didn't pass any.
But in that year, something else happened.

She met Prince Charles for the first time
at a party at her home.
Diana's sister, Sarah,
had been out with him.

Diana had always liked Charles.
She had a picture of him
in her bedroom at school.

When she left school,
she didn't know what to do.
She was sent to a school
in Switzerland.

Then when she came back,
she shared a flat with friends in London.
She still didn't know
what she wanted to do.
She did some cleaning for friends.
She worked as a waitress.

She wanted a job doing something
that she enjoyed.
Diana had always loved children,
so she became a full-time helper
in a nursery.

Then, in 1980, she met Prince Charles again,
at another party.
This was to change her life.

3 Romance

The papers started to write
about Charles' new girlfriend.
People began to wonder
if Charles and Diana would get married.
Photographers wanted pictures of Diana.
They would follow her in the street
when she was going to work.

The papers called her 'Shy Di'.
Diana would put her head down
because she didn't want her picture taken.
Diana didn't feel very confident about
herself and the way she looked.

She was tall, with blonde hair and blue eyes.
She was an 'English Rose',
but at only 18 years old, she didn't know
what all the fuss was about.
She thought she looked fat.

But people liked Diana because
she seemed ordinary.
When Diana and Charles got engaged,
people all over the world
looked forward to the wedding.

On TV, before the wedding,
Charles and Diana were asked
if they were in love.
Diana said 'Of course', but Charles said,
'Yes, whatever love is.'
Some people wondered what he meant.

But for many people, Charles and Diana's
romance was like a fairytale.
At last the Prince had found
his beautiful Princess.

There were pictures of the couple
in all the newspapers.

The wedding took place on 29 July 1981,
at St Paul's Cathedral in London.
Diana was only 20 years old.
Charles was 32.
About 750 million people all over the world
watched the wedding on TV.

It seemed that Charles and Diana
would live happily ever after.
Years later, Diana said:
'At the age of 19 you always think
you're prepared for everything.'
Diana was not prepared for what was ahead.

People all over the world watched on TV as Diana
married Charles.

4 The Fairy Tale Ends

In the early years of the marriage,
Diana and Charles seemed happy.
People had wondered
if the age gap would be a problem.
The papers had called her 'Disco Di'
because she loved going out and having fun.

Her children were born
soon after the marriage.
Prince William was born on 22 June 1982.
Prince Harry was born on 15 September 1984.

The papers loved to write about Diana.
She said later:
'... it started to focus very much on me
and I seemed to be on the front
of a newspaper every single day ...
and the higher the media put you,
the bigger the drop.'

Sometimes Diana could not take the attention.
She could not hide how she felt.
She could not be the perfect princess.

On a trip to Canada in 1986,
Diana looked ill and thin.
It was too much for her.
Inside she felt very, very low.
She fainted into Charles' arms.

The papers said that the marriage
was not going well.

The papers began to run stories about
how Diana and Charles were not happy together.
Only five years after they were married,
Diana and Charles started to spend
more and more time away from each other.

Diana made more time for her charity work.
She wanted to do good.
She wanted to help others.
Her charity work helped homeless people
and people with drug problems.
Diana seemed to sense the pain
that other people felt.

The photographers followed her everywhere.
She could use them to make people
aware of her charity work.

In 1987, she shook hands with
a person who had AIDS.
At this time, people did not know
much about AIDS.
Some people thought you could catch AIDS
by shaking hands with an AIDS patient.

The picture of Diana shaking hands
was in all the papers.
It made people think again.
It helped people to understand the illness.
In 1990, she opened the first centre
for women with AIDS.

She seemed to be the perfect princess.

5 Heartache for Diana

In her public life, Diana was giving
love out all the time to others.
She had glamour, beauty and style.
But her marriage to Charles
was falling apart.
The papers ran stories, saying that she was
seeing another man, James Hewitt.

When her father died in March 1992,
Diana was heart broken.
It seemed as if her life was falling apart.
In her pain, she had no-one to turn to.

Then a book went on sale.
It was called 'Diana, Her True Story'.
The book told how unhappy she was.
It said she had tried to kill herself.
At heart, Diana felt afraid and insecure.
The book told how she was ill with bulimia.
Bulimia is an illness
which makes you throw up your food.

The book was so shocking
that people wondered if it could be true.

In November 1992,
Charles and Diana went to Korea on a tour.
People could see how unhappy they were.
They hardly talked to each other.

It was the last time they were together
as a couple.

A month later, after 11 years of marriage,
Diana and Charles split up.

Diana lived alone
in Kensington Palace.

6 Telling All

In December 1993, a sad Diana said that
she was going to pull out of public life.
It seemed that being in the public eye
all the time was too much.
She cut back on her charity work.
However, she still led a very public life.

People always wanted to see
what she was wearing,
and what she looked like.
Diana had changed a lot from 'Shy Di'.
She was more confident
in front of the cameras.
People all over the world
thought that she was very beautiful.

Behind the pictures, Diana was still trying
to come to terms with
the end of her marriage.

Only a year after they split up,
Prince Charles went on TV.
He said that he had
never really loved Diana.
He said that he was pushed into the marriage.
He said that he had
always loved another woman.
Her name was Camilla Parker Bowles.

It seemed that Diana needed
to tell her own story.
In December 1995, Diana went on TV.

15 million people watched.
She talked about how her marriage fell apart.
She said:
'Well, there were three of us in the marriage,
so it was a bit crowded.'

She also said that she had had an affair.
She had fallen in love with James Hewitt.
She was heart broken
when he wrote about the affair.

Diana said she did have bulimia.
She said that she had been depressed
after her children were born.

'You wake up in the morning
feeling you didn't want to get out of bed –
you felt misunderstood
and very, very low in yourself.'

She said that she wanted to be
'a Queen of people's hearts.'
She said:
'. . . I know that I can give love for a minute,
for half an hour, for a day, for a month,
but I can give – I'm happy to do that,
and I want to do that.'

People liked her for being honest.
Diana spoke from her heart.
She said she didn't want a divorce
from Charles.
She didn't want her children to suffer.
She didn't want her boys to feel
the same pain she had felt as a child.

But three years later,
she agreed to divorce Charles.
What would she do now?

7 The Press

When Charles and Diana divorced,
Diana got £17 million.
She was allowed to share bringing up
her sons, but she could not have
the same royal title any more.
Now her title was
Diana, Princess of Wales.

But she was a star in her own right.
Whatever she did and wherever she went,
the photographers were always there.
Her face on the cover of a magazine
would help the magazine to sell thousands.

Often Diana wanted the press to be there.
She could use the newspapers to
tell everybody about her work.
When Diana watched a heart operation
the photographs of her were
on the front pages.
She was wearing a gown and mask.
She didn't mind these pictures being taken.

Diana used the press to tell people about her work.

But there were always photographers
who took pictures of her
when she didn't want them to.
One photographer took pictures of her
working out in a gym,
without her knowing.
She was wearing a leotard.
Again, the pictures were on the front page
of the newspapers.

Many people felt this was going too far,
to spy on her like this.
But people still bought the papers.

There were stories in the papers
that linked Diana with Will Carling,
the England rugby captain.
There were also stories about Diana
told by another man.
This man, Oliver Hoare, said that
she made late night phone calls to him.
He said she would phone him up,
then put the phone down when he answered.

Diana said she did not make these calls.
Nobody knew if it was true.
But people loved reading about it all
in the papers.

Photographers would follow her every day.
Sometimes it seemed
as if she had no private life.
But the press was useful to
highlight her public work.

She was the Head of the National AIDS Trust,
and the Great Ormond Street Children's Hospital
and four other charities.

One of Diana's wishes was
to see land mines banned.
When she went to Angola and Bosnia
to highlight her cause,
there were pictures and reports
about her visits in the papers and on TV.
In this way, she could use the press.

In New York, in June 1997,
she sold 79 of her dresses.
The sale made nearly £2 million.
The money went to cancer and AIDS charities.

It seemed that Diana
was making a new life for herself.
She also had a new man in her life.
Maybe this relationship could work?

8 The Last Summer

It is the end of the summer of 1997.
Her last summer.
Diana has never looked more beautiful.
She seems to be happy for
the first time in years.
The man she is with is Dodi Al Fayed.
He is the son of one of her father's friends.
Dodi's father owns Harrods.

In the papers there have been pictures
of Diana and Dodi on holiday.
Diana and Dodi didn't know
the pictures were being taken.
The photographers are always there,
trying to take pictures of them all the time.

Diana seems very happy.
At last she seems to have found real love.

It is Saturday 30 August 1997.
Diana is wearing a new ring.
One that Dodi has given her.
The ring cost £130,000.

Diana and Dodi go to the Ritz Hotel in Paris.
After their dinner,
Diana and Dodi leave the hotel.
Diana, Dodi, the driver and the bodyguard
get into the black Mercedes.
But they have been spotted
by photographers.
Trying to escape,
they speed through the streets.
The car is going faster and faster.
The photographers are chasing them.
They want more pictures of Diana and Dodi.

The car is going too fast
as it enters an underpass.
The driver has lost control.
At 121 mph, the car crashes into a wall.

The first people to get to the car
are the photographers.
Dodi and the driver are dead.
The bodyguard has terrible injuries.

Diana is still alive. Just.
Her chest has been crushed.
Her beautiful face is unharmed.

Before the police arrive,
the photographers start taking pictures,
to sell to the newspapers.
Diana has to be cut free from the car.

On the way to the hospital,
her heart stops beating.
The doctors start it again.
In the hospital, the doctors battle to save
the Queen of people's hearts.
Diana has been in an operating theatre before.
But this time, she is the patient.
For hours, the doctors try
to get her heart to beat.

She dies at 4.41am.

The news of her death shocks the world.
How can Diana die?

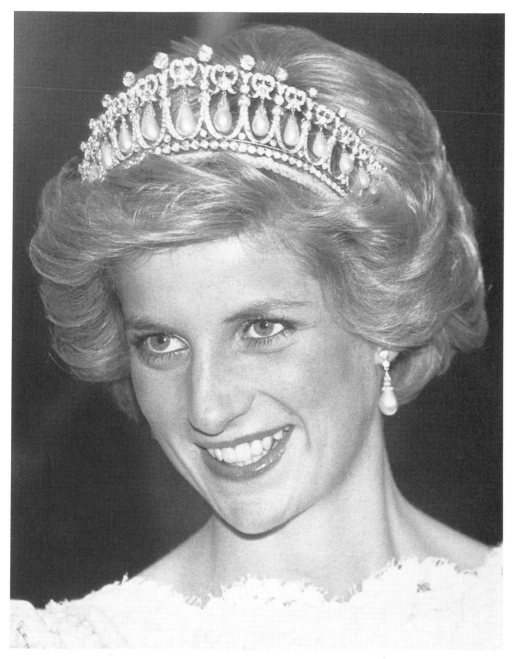

Diana, Princess of Wales: July 1961 – August 1997.

9 The People's Princess

People tried to work out why she died.

Why was the car going so fast?
Was it the driver? He had been drinking.
Was the press to blame?
They always wanted more pictures of her.
Was the public to blame?
They always wanted to read about her.

We may never know
why the accident happened.
But the children who
were helped by Diana's work
at Great Ormond Street Hospital
will always remember her.
People from the National AIDS Trust
will always remember her.

To them, and to many others,
Diana was the People's Princess.

Diana's grave is at Althorp House.
It is on the island where she played
as a young girl with her brother.